CGP

Key Stage Three

Spelling, Punctuation & Grammar

Answer Book

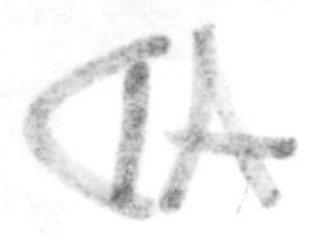

Contents

Published by CGP

ISBN: 978 1 78294 116 3

Website: www.cgpbooks.co.uk

Printed by Elanders Ltd, Newcastle upon Tyne.
Clipart from Corel®

Based on the classic CGP style created by Richard Parsons.

Answers

Section One — Spelling

Page 1 — Plurals

Q1 **a)** benches
b) sweets
c) dogs
d) witnesses
e) files
f) buses
g) foxes

Q2 **a)** The monkeys poked me in the kidneys.
b) Their jerseys got stuck in the chimneys.
c) The boys found a way of mending the toys.

Q3 Plurals that should end '-ies':
babies, rubies, stories, skies, flies.
Plurals that should end '-s':
subways, chimneys, keys, sprays, valleys.

Q4 My favourite animal is a donkey. One of the reasons I like donkeys is that they have great long ears. Their favourite hobbies are eating and cooking — they take lots of meat and vegetables, and make the most delicious meals. I used to keep my donkeys in fields, but ever since it rained cats and dogs last Tuesday, I have to keep them all in boxes. I don't think they like it much in there, but I've promised to give them all pet puppies if they behave.

Page 2 — Plurals

Q5 **a)** Do you ever go to any school discos?
b) They sold banjos and other musical instruments.
c) Have you taken any photos today?
d) I sing alto, but Sally and Karen are sopranos.

Q6 **a)** Our heroes ate mangoes on the volcanoes.
(hero, mango, volcano)
b) The ships lost their cargoes when they were hit by torpedoes.
(cargo, torpedo)
c) The heavenly echoes made the angels drop their haloes.
(echo, halo)

Q7 **a)** Any shop that sells televisions will probably sell radios and stereos too.
(The plurals can be in any order.)
b) Some people think zoos are cruel.
c) My dog weighs about six kilos.
d) My childhood heroes were mostly athletes.
e) If I'm going to sell vegetables, I'll have to be able to spell 'tomatoes' and 'potatoes'.
(The plurals can be in any order.)
f) The dance classes all take place in different studios.

Page 3 — Plurals

Q8 The wives in the village had begun putting their loaves of bread up on high shelves because the local wolves kept acting like thieves and stealing them. These fierce animals frightened the calves in the hills, which meant they kept running off the cliffs in panic. The loss of cattle was threatening the lives of the chief's people because they were running out of meat. Something had to be done.

"We'll have to get the army of dwarves in," said the chief.

The dwarves sharpened their knives, wrapped themselves in thick scarves and made disguises out of leaves as they waited for the wolves. However, the wolves were too clever — they used the panicked calves to distract the dwarves and then stole the loaves in the confusion.

Q9 **a)** men
b) women
c) children
d) mice
e) teeth
f) geese

Q10

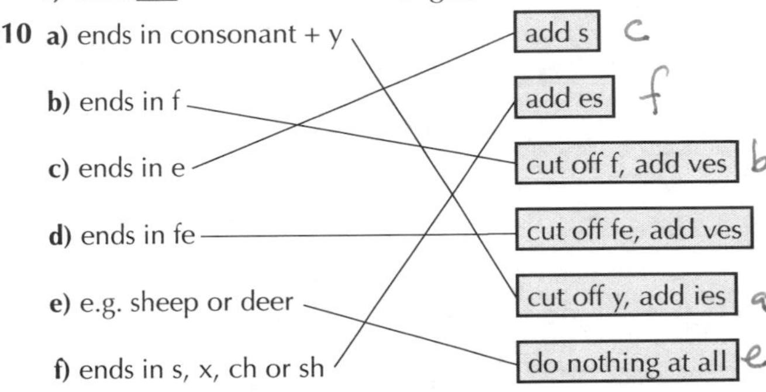

Page 4 — Prefixes

Q1 **a)** unhappy
b) inactive
c) invisible
d) uncover
e) undress
f) unfair

Q2 **a)** irresistible
b) illegible
c) impossible
d) impatient
e) immature
f) illogical

Q3 **a)** It's going to be impossible to finish all this work in an hour.
b) Doing things in this order is illogical.
c) I'm trying to diet, but that ice cream is just irresistible.
d) "You're so immature," she snapped at the boys who were trying to put a worm down her neck.
e) Don't be so impatient! She'll be here in a minute.
f) I can't read this — your writing is completely illegible.

Q4 **a)** displease
b) unnecessary
c) immoral
d) misunderstood
e) disagree
f) illegal
g) indiscreet
h) irresponsible

Page 5 — Prefixes

Q5 **a)** disappear — (reappear)
b) reuse — (abuse, disuse, misuse, overuse)
c) precook — (overcook, recook)
d) replace — (displace, misplace)
e) supermarket — (hypermarket, remarket, upmarket)
f) unable — (disable, enable)
g) disorder — (reorder)
h) undo — (outdo, overdo, redo, underdo)
i) preview — (interview, overview, review)
j) underarm — (disarm, forearm, overarm, rearm)

Q6 **a)** Abdul's singing made him an international superstar.
b) The weather forecast says it will rain all day.
c) I always use the microwave — it's much quicker than the oven.

Answers

d) David needed to refresh his memory by rereading this page.
e) My parents bought me a new bicycle for my birthday.
f) The source of the gossip was unknown.
g) I have to disagree with you — Cola Bottles are much better than Strawberry Laces.

Q7

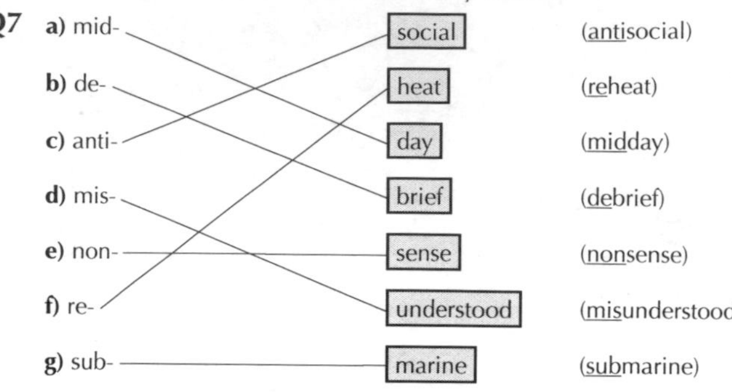

'mid-' means middle
'de-' means undo or reverse
'anti-' means against or opposite
'mis-' means wrongly or badly
'non-' means not
're-' means again
'sub-' means under

Page 6 — Suffixes

Q1 a) curable
b) videoing
c) excited
d) noticing
e) responsible
f) shaking
g) arguable
h) reversible
i) braking

Q2

Root Word	-ed	-ing	-able
describe	described	describing	describable
squeeze	squeezed	squeezing	squeezable
achieve	achieved	achieving	achievable
admire	admired	admiring	admirable
manage	managed	managing	manageable
adore	adored	adoring	adorable
believe	believed	believing	believable

Q3 a) She was careful not to disturb anyone as she crept in.
b) At ten to four, everyone had gone home and the school was peaceful.
c) He desperately wanted to be allowed to go on the trip.
d) Finishing the race in such a short time was a tremendous achievement.
e) Don't throw that away — it could be useful.
f) He was a good advertisement for his school.
g) You must measure ingredients accurately or the recipe won't work.

Page 7 — Suffixes

Q4 a) His behaviour is incredible.
b) Your cheek is unbelievable.
c) Your writing is only just legible.
d) The whole essay was barely readable.
e) It was terrible to see him so ill.
f) We all felt utterly miserable.
g) It's possible that I made a mistake.
h) He's a very reliable chap.
i) Who's responsible for this mess?
j) There are several identifiable problems.
k) The meal was completely inedible.
l) It was a thoroughly enjoyable evening.

Q5 a) His habit of keeping skunks made him rather unemployable.
b) Her ambition was to start her own hamster-grooming business.
c) He hated being reminded of his win in the prettiest baby contest.
d) Their neighbour often played his piano very loudly.
e) Peter enjoyed dressing up when he was younger.
f) The dog wasn't allowed on the chair until her coat had dried.
g) We need someone reliable to do our homework for us.
h) Ellie decided she fancied some chocolate.

Q6 Adjectives

happy	happier	happiest
lazy	lazier	laziest
flashy	flashier	flashiest
heavy	heavier	heaviest

Verbs:

justify	justifies	justified
multiply	mutiplies	multiplied
qualify	qualifies	qualified
hurry	hurries	hurried

Page 8 — Suffixes

Q7 a) "This parrot is quite annoying," said the pirate.
b) Hannah is supplying me with the answers to the questions.
c) Everyone at the disco was partying away all evening.
d) I'm frying some bacon for us to have for breakfast.
e) There's no point in denying it.
f) Tom soon found that copying his brother wasn't a good idea.
g) Liam thought about applying for the chef position.
h) I'm trying to understand how you worked this out.

Q8

Root Word	-ed	-ing
tag	tagged	tagging
bat	batted	batting

Answers

Root Word	-ed	-ing
prefer	preferred	preferring
hum	hummed	humming
prod	prodded	prodding
step	stepped	stepping
limit	limited	limiting
jog	jogged	jogging
visit	visited	visiting
commit	committed	committing

Page 9 — Suffixes

Q9 **a)** Alice was having an upsetting day because the new project she was starting was very difficult.
b) Jack was distracted by gazing out of the window.
c) I would have preferred chocolate, but Bill only offered me vanilla.
d) "That's the craziest thing I've ever heard," shouted Josh.
e) Stop wasting my time — I am exhausted.
f) Shutting my shop early meant I could get some gardening done.
g) Jenny was hoping she would be able to go running after work.
h) After she had emptied the bins, Aisha tried to fix the tap.
i) Stopping himself from shouting at his dad proved very difficult.
j) Matt was feeling very bored after he had studied for three hours.

Q10 **a)** His thumb just fited in the plughole, but then it was traped. (fitted, trapped)
b) She was so excitted that she began hoping up and down on the spot. (excited, hopping)
c) They hopped to find homes for all the baby rabbits before the next lot arrivved. (hoped, arrived)
d) When they saw the look on her face, they wishhed they'd stoped. (wished, stopped)
e) He fell when he sawwed off the branch he was siting on. (sawed, sitting)

Page 10 — Comparing Things

Q1 **a)** faster **b)** heavier **c)** prettier **d)** bigger **e)** happier **f)** wetter

Q2 **a)** Chocolate is more delicious than sprouts.
b) Cities are usually more crowded than villages.
c) Learning grammar is more boring than watching paint dry.

Q3 **a)** Kitchen chairs are less comfortable than armchairs.
b) The view downstairs is less beautiful than the one upstairs.
c) Winter is less colourful than Autumn.
d) David is less intelligent than Susan.

Q4 **a)** Apples are more healthy / healthier than crisps.
b) Max is more successful in maths exams than science exams.
c) This year's fireworks more fantastic than last year's.
d) Jack is better at baking than Jenny.
e) I like my tea weaker than Matt does.
f) I wish I could spend less time at school.
g) Running is quicker than walking.
h) I am worse at spelling than my sister.
i) Sarah's shoes are newer than Richard's.
j) Revising is more fun than going to the cinema.

Page 11 — Saying Something is the Most or Least

Q1 **a)** My phone is the most expensive thing I own.
b) Princess Perfect is the most beautiful.
c) The Christmas party was the merriest.
d) Motorways are usually the widest roads.
e) Football is the most fun sport.

Q2 **a)** This necklace is the least valuable piece of jewellery I own.
b) Anchovies are the least popular pizza topping.
c) Adam is the least talkative cat I have ever met.
d) Billy's flat is the least peaceful one in the building.
e) Alice is the least funny person I know.

Q3 **a)** highest **b)** emptiest **c)** saddest **d)** thickest **e)** driest **f)** safest

Q4

Adjective	Comparative	Superlative
little	less	least
much/many	more	most
bad	worse	worst
good	better	best

Page 12 — Silent Letters

Q1 It was the first day of the Christmas holidays and Mary was enjoying not being at school. She spent the morning watching her mum cooking. She liked to listen to her mum singing while she worked.

After her mum had finished, they spent an hour wrapping presents. They used scissors to cut the paper and then fastened the gifts with tape. Then they made some cards, which took ages. Mary drew a nativity scene for her dad and a picture of a castle for her brother. She sprayed perfume on them to make them scented and then put them in their envelopes.

Silent 't'	Silent 'c'	Silent 'h'
Christmas, listen, fastened, castle	scissors, scene, scented	Christmas, school, while, hour, which

Q2 **a)** knowledge **b)** conscience **c)** doubt **d)** could **e)** fascinate **f)** subtle **g)** ghost **h)** answer **i)** kneel **j)** honest **k)** wrong **l)** thumb

Q3 **a)** The knight used his sword to kill the dragon.
b) I need to talk to someone about my debt.
c) Chemistry is the hardest science lesson.

Answers

d) Emma's father walked her down the aisle on her wedding day.
e) John wanted to make a sign that would show people where to go.
f) Two of the explorers left the group to search for the lost tomb.
g) The whole football team started lifting weights to develop their muscles.

Page 13 — Vowel Sounds

Q1 **a)** different **b)** dictionary **c)** instrument **d)** original **e)** interest **f)** interrupt **g)** primary **h)** marvellous **i)** vegetable **j)** frighten **k)** natural **l)** parliament

Unstressed 'a'	Unstressed 'e'
dictionary, original, primary, vegetable, natural, parliament	different, instrument, interest, interrupt, marvellous, frighten

Q2 **a)** carr(o)t **b)** tot(a)lly **c)** h(o)riz(o)n **d)** lant(e)rn **e)** necess(a)ry **f)** deliv(e)ry **g)** fatt(e)ning **h)** r(i)dicul(ou)s **i)** mem(o)ry **j)** centr(a)l **k)** gov(e)rnm(e)nt **l)** alph(a)bet **m)** jewell(e)ry **n)** doct(o)r **o)** fact(o)ry

Q3 **a)** They said it was voluntary, but I don't remember volunteering.
b) If the ball goes over the boundary, you score a four.
c) She desperately wanted a part in the play.
d) He always felt like giggling in the library.
e) I generally prefer football to rugby.
f) I always get separated from my friends because I don't pay enough attention.

Page 14 — Hard and Soft 'c' Sounds

Q1 **a)** The chemist cuddled his cat in the middle of the (c)emetery.
b) Cairo and Canberra are capital (c)ities on different continents.
c) A (c)ircle of clouds collected around the (c)entre of the canyon.
d) Captain Clark is a character who keeps lots of cats.

Q2 Words beginning with a 'soft c':
cymbal, century, ceiling, cycling, cement, circus, cinder

Q3 **a)** acceptable **b)** license **c)** accidentally **d)** muscle **e)** pronunciation **f)** receive **g)** experience **h)** expensive **i)** sensible **j)** innocence

Q4 **a)** serviceable **b)** servicing **c)** fiercely **d)** fiercest **e)** priceless **f)** spicy **g)** pronounced **h)** replacement

Page 15 — i Before e Rule

Q1 **a)** deceive **b)** achieve **c)** piece **d)** receiver **e)** ceiling **f)** receipt **g)** diesel **h)** thief **i)** neighbour **j)** hygiene **k)** relief **l)** weight

Q2 I believe that the 'i before e' rule is the chief of all spelling rules. It has achieved such popularity that it is perceived as being flawless. However, it is actually a deceitful and mischievous rule because it has a few exceptions. Despite this minor flaw, you shouldn't reject it as either ancient or a useless counterfeit. It might be a bit weird, but as long as you learn the exceptions, it can be a very efficient spelling reminder.

Q3 **a)** vacancies **b)** fancied **c)** policies **d)** juiciest
These words show that the spelling rules for adding suffixes are more important than the 'i before e' rule. This means that for the words in this question, the 'i before e' rule doesn't work.
(Or any sensible answer with a similar conclusion.)

Q4 Words that don't obey the 'i before e' rule:
fancied, species, diet, protein, friend, seize

Page 16 — Commonly Misused Words

Q1 "There's absolutely no way I'm going skydiving," said James. "No one will be able to persuade me. I wish everyone would just stop pestering me."
"But we need someone brave — like you," said Jenny. "There isn't anyone else."
"I'm sorry, but there's nothing I can do," said James firmly. "If nobody else will do it then you'll have to think of something else."

Q2 **a)** Is there any way / some way we can have lunch early today?
b) There must be somebody who's interested in his stamp collection.
c) Skeletons don't have any body.
d) We need to think of something to do during the school holidays.
e) Louise looked everywhere for her favourite stripy tights.
f) It was raining heavily, but we went to the beach anyway.
g) I'm sorry, but there isn't really anything I can do to help.
h) We need to find somewhere with some shade for our picnic.

Q3 **a)** Maybe we should save this for a rainy day.
b) "Guess who I ran into at the supermarket?"
c) I only popped in to get some milk.
d) There may be a surprise party for Ted's birthday.

Page 17 — Commonly Misused Words

Q4 **a)** There is a lot of evidence to suggest that lollipops are better than ice creams.
b) Thank you for returning my fairy wings.
c) I don't have too many shoes; in fact, I don't have enough.

Answers

Q5 a) Mohammed devised a way of teaching his rabbit to do his homework for him.
b) Aaron found his homework much easier after he had taken Charlotte's advice.
c) I'm going to be late for netball practice.
d) Tricia's taxi is licensed to carry four passengers.
e) The photo on my driving licence is so embarrassing.
f) I would advise you to stop insulting your boss if you want to keep your job.
g) Mr Hunt began to practise his Christmas carols in May.

Q6 a) past adjective
Any sentence where 'past' is used correctly as an adjective:
E.g. Dad drove past the school.
Past pupils were better behaved.
b) passed verb
Any sentence where 'passed' is used correctly as a verb:
E.g. He passed me the ball.
I passed the gym on the way to class.

Q7 a) It doesn't seem to have any effect on me.
b) I'm sorry, we don't accept credit cards.
c) Playing more sport will definitely affect your health.
d) Alan likes all sweets, except orange-flavoured ones.

Page 18 — Commonly Misused Words

Q8

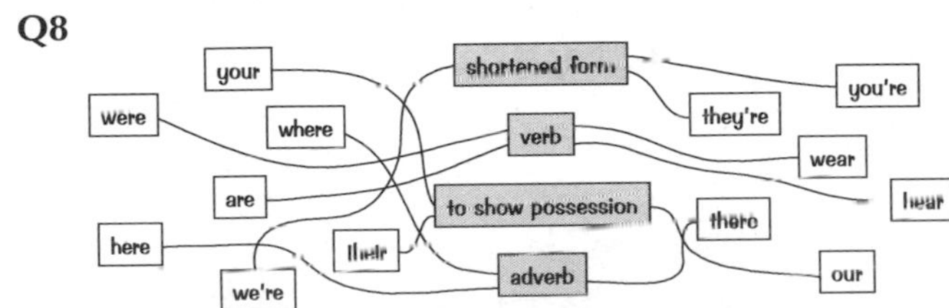

Q9

	Definition
by	next to **or** because of
buy	pay for something
bye	shortened form of goodbye

	Definition
to	towards
too	too much **or** also
two	the number 2

Q10 a) All of my friends are off on holiday. I was scared of being lonely, but now I think I'm better off without any of them.
b) The cat jumped off the pillow, so I got out of bed, turned off the light, and went to sleep. I dreamt of a room full of flowers.

Q11 a) Mr Clarke was thorough when he went through Lee's homework.
b) We went through the tunnel, though it took longer.
c) Even though she looked for ages, Sam's search wasn't thorough enough to find the remote.

Page 19 — Commonly Misused Words

Q12 It was a dark, cold night. The whether was horrible and the woulds around the house were wild and stormy. Olivia lay in bed and wished for some piece and quite.
"I wish that rain wood stop," she said allowed.
As the rain died down, Olivia started to wonder weather she could sneak downstairs for a peace of chocolate cake. She hadn't been aloud a slice at tea because she'd argued with her brother.
He could be quiet a pain in the neck...

weather / whether — quiet / quite
woods / would — aloud / allowed
peace / piece

Q13 a) One of my teeth is loose, but I don't want to lose it.
b) If any more frogs get loose, I may lose my job at the zoo.

Q14 a) Can you pass me them crisps? (those)
b) Whose going to take me to hockey practice tonight? (Who's)
c) Who's stinky socks are those on the kitchen floor? (Whose)

Q15 a) You can borrow this DVD if you lend me one in return.
b) I brought a packed lunch, but Ahmed bought his at the shops.
c) If I'm going to learn all this before the exam, someone will have to teach me really well.

Page 20 — Mixed Questions

Q1 a) boxes
b) agencies
c) feet
d) halves
e) parts
f) fish
(Don't write 'fishes' — it's really old-fashioned.)
g) journeys
h) leaves

Q2 a) subconsciously
b) inaccurately
c) disagreement
d) misdialled
e) resetting
f) unhappiest
g) predefined
h) overstaying

Q3

Adjective	Comparative	Superlative
smart	smarter	smartest
silly	sillier	silliest
fat	fatter	fattest
late	later	latest
funny	funnier	funniest
brave	braver	bravest
far	further	furthest
mad	madder	maddest

Answers

Page 21 — Mixed Questions

Q4
- **a)** biscuit
- **b)** loving
- **c)** knives
- **d)** cried
- **e)** receive
- **f)** adjacent
- **g)** shield
- **h)** embarrass
- **i)** manageable
- **j)** travelling
- **k)** rhyme
- **l)** welcome

Q5
- **a)** I've forgotten to double the 'p' of 'snip'. If the root word ends in a single consonant and the suffix ('-ing') begins with a vowel, the last letter of the root word is usually doubled.
- **b)** I've forgotten to drop the 'e' of 'hope'. If the root word ends in an 'e' and the suffix ('-ing') begins with a vowel, then the 'e' of the root word is usually dropped.
- **c)** I've forgotten that, in English, a 'q' is nearly always followed by a 'u'.
- **d)** 'Dog's' is a possessive form, or a shortened form of 'dog is'. It isn't a plural form. I should have written 'dogs'.
- **e)** The 'i before e rule' only works when the 'ie' sound rhymes with bee. The 'ie' sound in neighbour sounds like 'ay', so it's 'ei' not 'ie'.
- **f)** Most words ending in 'o' just add 's' for the plural. Words like 'tomatoes' and 'potatoes' are the exceptions.

Page 22 — Mixed Questions

Q6
- **a)** accommodation
- **b)** rhythm
- **c)** embarrass
- **d)** queue
- **e)** fought
- **f)** strength
- **g)** eventually
- **h)** rogue
- **i)** enough
- **j)** necessary
- **k)** aeroplane
- **l)** catalogue
- **m)** address
- **n)** Wednesday

Q7
- **a)** motion
- **b)** politician
- **c)** collision
- **d)** occasion
- **e)** optician
- **f)** attention
- **g)** population

Q8

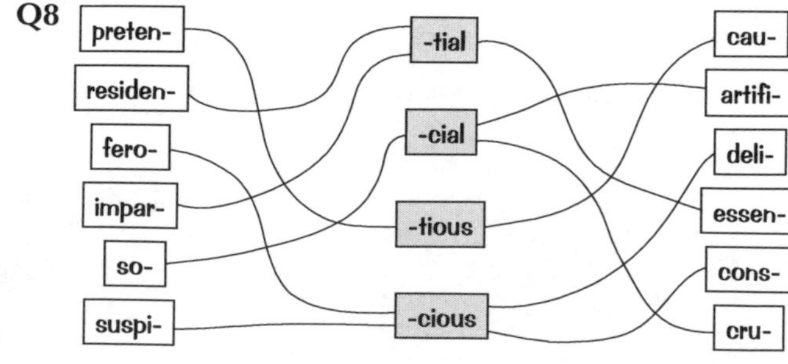

Page 23 — Mixed Questions

Q9 Bob Angelo has been drawing sketches for years. He is probably most famous for his illustration of a parade in the foreground of Venice Cathedral. This pencil drawing highlights his incredible skill, and is currently on exhibition at the British Gallery.

Occasionally, I visit the city square, where you can see all the impressive government buildings. It's usually full of people, walking and chatting. The atmosphere's brilliant. My favourite part is definitely the cathedral, which is one of the grandest I've ever seen. The stained glass windows are especially beautiful. There's also a temporary coffee shop there, where you're guaranteed to find delicious cakes and even tastier / more tasty hot chocolate. The neighbouring chapel was built at a separate time from the cathedral and is famous for having nuns buried inside.

Yesterday the government was still fiercely refusing to comment specifically on the matter. However, an official spokesman said: "The Prime Minister has no reason to believe that the Secretary of State acted inappropriately. Furthermore, he is an experienced and conscientious member of the cabinet at the height of his career." Other supporters of the Secretary have also confirmed their desire to keep him in office. Unfortunately this issue is not likely to disappear any time soon, and political advisors are warning that new strategies may be necessary if they are to gain enough support for the Secretary to retain his job. In parliament, opposition MPs are calling for explanations, and asking questions about the "outrageous cover-up".

Section Two — Punctuation

Page 24 — Punctuating Sentences

Q1
- **a)** Tyrone asked if the cake was nice.
- **b)** Are you going to Shelley's party?
- **c)** Julian wished he was better at chess.
- **d)** Would you like ketchup or brown sauce?
- **e)** Adam wanted to know if the bread was mouldy.

Q2 My name is Beatrix. There aren't many famous people called Beatrix, but the Netherlands used to be ruled by Queen Beatrix. Her reign lasted for over thirty years, until she abdicated in April 2013.

Beatrix is also the name of a famous writer that I love called Beatrix Potter. She was an English author who wrote about animals and the countryside. Her most famous character is named Peter Rabbit — he's a rabbit that gets into lots of trouble.

However, my favourite story about rabbits is called 'Watership Down'. People often question if a book all about rabbits would be enjoyable. Interestingly, everyone I know thinks it's amazing. Unfortunately, it's not by Beatrix Potter.

Page 25 — Commas

Q1
- **a)** I'd like to see Jane, Phil and Peter after assembly.
- **b)** Mary found it difficult to concentrate. Nevertheless, she struggled on.
- **c)** He's certain it's the right thing to do. However, I'm not so sure.
- **d)** Ice cream and chocolate sauce, fish and chips, and bangers and mash are all good combinations.
- **e)** Metals are good conductors, but non-metals are good insulators.
- **f)** Peter's favourite colours are pink, dark yellow and green.
- **g)** There will be some big news this week, so be sure to check the noticeboards.

Answers

h) We could go to bed, or we could watch another film.

Q2 a) My great grandmother, who's ninety-six, can remember the war.
b) Mr Green's car, which is very new and shiny, has got a big scratch on it.
c) Johnny, one of my best friends, is a very bad dancer.
d) Anaconda, which is a very long word, is extremely difficult to spell.

Q3 Mr Hyde, who is my teacher, brought his rabbit into school yesterday. It has fluffy, long, white fur and is very friendly. I don't really like rabbits, but I loved Mr Hyde's rabbit. It was so cute, with its floppy ears, big eyes and long whiskers. Mr Hyde even let me hold the rabbit for a bit. However, I was worried that it might be dirty, so I made sure I washed my hands afterwards.

Page 26 — Colons and Semicolons

Q1 a) Jackie loves Christmas: she always gets loads of presents.
b) Rosie was giggling: Simon's joke was really funny.
c) Dogs are very lazy: all they do is sleep all day.
d) There are two major problems with the act: the jokes aren't funny, and we can't hear him.

Q2 a) Ben has blue shoes; Tony's shoes are red.
b) Shopping is very tiring; it's probably more tiring than playing football.
c) I enjoy many hobbies: playing the violin, which my mum got me into; playing chess, as it's a good mental challenge; and football, because it's a good way to keep fit.
d) You are very good at playing the piano; you must practise a lot.

Q3 In **a)** the two clauses are of equal importance and are linked, but it's not clear how — the sheriff might be the cause of the street emptying, or he might be walking into town because the street has emptied. In **b)** the second clause clearly explains the first — the street has emptied because the sheriff walked into town. (Or any similar answer that explains the differences of using colons and semicolons.)

Q4 a) You'll need to bring: a packed lunch, drinks, spare clothes and a sunhat.
b) We've had to cancel after-school hockey practice: there's a shortage of light.
c) My parents had to go to a meeting with Mrs Lawrence, the Head of English; Mr Kemp, my headteacher; Mr Burton, my head of year; and Jane Wood, the school counsellor.

Page 27 — Brackets and Dashes

Q1 a) It was too hot (between 32 °C and 34 °C) to do any exercise.
b) The twins (Miles and Maisy) were very loud.
c) You should read the FAQs (frequently asked questions) before contacting us.
d) My birthday (26th July) is my favourite day of the year.
e) Pumas (a type of big cat) are very good hunters.

Q2 a) The swimmers were very calm — until they saw the shark.
b) The model — an enormous dinosaur skeleton — was a big hit at the museum.
c) Johnny was not being sarcastic at all — or was he?
d) The Battle of Titan Hill was the most important battle in November — if not the whole war.

Q3 a) Everyone was very relaxed — until they noticed the huge spider.
b) My new neighbours (Sue and Morris) are very friendly. (You could also use dashes instead of brackets in this sentence, but brackets would be better.)
c) ASAP (as soon as possible) is a very common acronym. (You could also use dashes instead of brackets in this sentence, but brackets would be better.)
d) I always get lots of cards on February 14th (Valentine's Day).
e) The room was completely empty — or so we thought.

Q4 a) True
b) False
c) False
d) True
e) True
f) False

Page 28 — Hyphens

Q1 a) My dad says he's having a mid-life crisis.
b) That wouldn't happen in real life.
c) I'm a part-time employee.
d) My parrot is twenty-seven years old.

Q2 a) ex-husband
b) self-confident
c) extraordinary
d) re-emerge
e) reread
f) underestimate

Q3

Word	This word needs a hyphen because...
re-cover	otherwise it can be confused with 'recover'.
pro-British	the root word starts with a capital letter.
co-own	the root word starts with the same letter that the prefix ends with.

Q4 a) A shark that eats people.
b) A man who is eating shark meat.
c) A man who sells new cars.
d) A man who is new at his job in car sales.
e) A group of kittens that are five years old.
f) Five kittens that are one year old.

Page 29 — Apostrophes

Q1 a) I think that's the best thing that ever happened to me.
b) You don't all have to shout at once.
c) You're the fastest worker I ever saw.
d) When they finish, they'll come over here.
e) I can't believe you remembered my birthday.
f) Do you know who's won the cup?

Answers

Q2 a) can't
b) he'll
c) That's
d) We're
e) doesn't

Q3

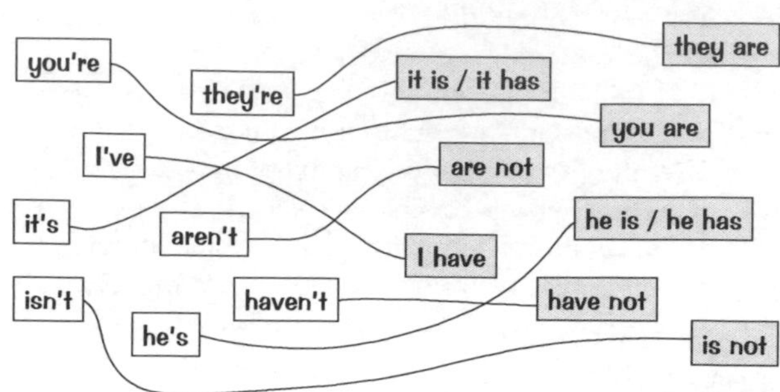

Q4 a) Let's have fishfingers and peas for tea tonight.
b) We'll have to see if Mum lets us stay up to watch it.
c) Let's go out to the cinema.

Page 30 — Apostrophes

Q5 a) Pass Mum's bag over.
b) Bill's football kit is filthy.
c) Ann is Elizabeth's mum.
d) Leave Jack's things alone.
e) It's the ladies' turn to go first.
f) That's the mice's house.
g) Put all the babies' pictures together.
h) Mrs Jackson's class is taking assembly.
i) Give me Jane's homework.
j) Copy the work out of Tom's book.
k) The other children's parents were nice.
l) The women's dresses were all the same.

Q6 a) the man's head
b) Nat's football
c) Carlos's scar
d) the horse's leg
e) the video's label
f) the chef's hat

Q7 a) one
b) more than one
c) more than one
d) one

Page 31 — Apostrophes

Q8 a) I don't know why men's feet tend to be bigger than women's.
b) Our house is near the airport, so we can hear the aircraft's engines all night.
c) The sponsored walk raised £300 for the children's playground.
d) The sheep's wool was very soft.

Q9 a) I've got my lunch, but I didn't pick yours up.
b) Jon said the book was his, but Sunita said it was hers.
c) I'm sure it's hurt; it's got its wing hanging down.
d) Tom's drawing is bigger, but I think mine's better.
e) They'll perform theirs first, and then we'll do ours when they're finished.

Q10 a) It's a shame that the school's hamster escaped.
b) It's quite a rare breed, I think.
c) I think its cage was broken.
d) It's got a new one now.
e) Hopefully it's more secure than the last one.
f) The school says it's tested it thoroughly.

Page 32 — Inverted Commas

Q1 a) "Have you got the sheepdog back yet?" asked Jeremy.
b) "I'm sorry," I replied, "I don't know the answer to that."
c) The children looked bored, so I asked, "Would you like to go to the park?"
d) "Stop pulling my hair!" screamed Alice.
e) "Naz, if you don't give Adam's shoes back," he yelled, "you'll regret it."
f) "Where," she asked, in a moment of confusion, "is my handbag?"

Q2 a) "What would you like to do this weekend?" asked Melanie.
b) "Please remind me," said Tim, "that I need to be home for tea at six."
c) "I can't do it!" exclaimed Julia.
d) "Personally," added Steve, "I'm not really a big fan of vegetables."

Q3 As soon as Sophie went downstairs, her dad asked her if she was all right.
"I'm fine," said Sophie. "It's just these horrible nightmares." She asked her dad if she looked tired.
"I don't think so," her dad replied, although he thought she looked exhausted.
"Maybe I'll take a nap later — hopefully that will give me a bit of colour," mumbled Sophie as she left.

Page 33 — Inverted Commas

Q4 a) David asked what kind of cake he should bake.
b) Emily said that I should meet her mother.
c) Mr Clarkson replied that he didn't know the answer to that.

Q5 a) "I don't understand what you're saying," said Jamie.
b) "Can you give us directions to the beach?" asked my aunt.
c) "I'll pick you up at nine o'clock," agreed Ben's dad.

Q6 a) "Elton John's a ruddy marvellous singer," he said passionately.
b) "Do you think white stilettos are classy?" she asked sarcastically.
c) "Elvis is not dead. He's just resting," she said seriously.
d) "My uncle used to be a rabbit," he said apologetically.
e) "Don't ever borrow my fishnets again!" she shouted angrily.

Page 34 — Mixed Questions

Q1 Last summer, we went on holiday to Spain. We went in July, so the weather was beautiful. My favourite thing about Spain is the food. I love the traditional Spanish dishes like paella. The best place to try paella is in Madrid. One weekend we went there to meet some friends — the Knox family. We ate at a restaurant called 'Tavernita'. I get on really well with the Knox family, especially the two older boys (Johnny and Ollie). It's a shame that we only ever really see them at Christmas.

Answers

Q2 **a)** How can you say that?
b) Watch out!
c) Is this legal?
d) Where is the emergency stop button?
e) Empty your pockets right now!
f) What is the meaning of this?

Q3 **a)** Let me know if you want to come.
b) My elder sister, who is a nurse, has a lot of experience in this area.
c) There are many new songs, several of which are different from the old stuff.
d) I met a lot of interesting people, some of whom I really liked.
e) My computer, which is really old, isn't working this morning.
f) She mentioned several things that were bothering her.

Q4 **a)** "There's something else you don't know: I hate rice pudding."
b) "I'll tell you how the other team beat us: they cheated from start to finish."
c) You will need the following: sugar, egg whites, cream, melted chocolate.

Page 35 — Mixed Questions

Q5 **a)** True **b)** False **c)** False **d)** True **e)** False **f)** True

Q6 **a)** People often use 'P.S.' (postscript) without knowing what it stands for.
b) Dave (my sister's boyfriend) bought me a book for my birthday.
c) The Declaration of Independence is celebrated on Independence Day (4th July).
d) Dodos (now extinct) were large birds that couldn't fly.

Q7 **a)** The pro-British forces needed permission to re-enter international waters.
b) If you send me the forms, I'll re-sign them for the twenty-second time.
c) The eight-year-old girls are celebrating their eighth birthdays today.

Q8 **a)** I've got Jamie's trainers in my bag, but I can't give them back yet.
b) We're on Marcus's team, but he's not as good as the other teams' captains.
c) I'm not sure I'd like the job she's just been offered.

Page 36 — Mixed Questions

Q9 **a)** Mr Burns interrupted to ask if we had done all the questions.
b) "Will you look after my bag whilst I go and order?" asked Heather.
c) "You're so annoying!" exclaimed my sister.
d) "I'm going to the shop," said Aaron, "I need some chocolate."

Q10 Last week, we went on a school trip to France. We left on Wednesday morning (the 27th) and returned on Saturday evening (the 30th).

"Have you got your lunch?" my mum asked on the morning of the trip. She told me to check the letter from school to see if I had forgotten anything. It said that I would need the following: a waterproof jacket, spending money and some spare clothes.

My teacher, Mr Jones, organised the trip. He made sure it was cheap, but the school said its budget wouldn't cover flights. We went by ferry instead, which was fun — until it got rough. Lots of people were ill: Jimmy, my ex-boyfriend, was sick on my shoes; as was Karen, the girl who sat in front of me; and Ralph, who'd had too many milkshakes.

Section Three — Grammar: Basics

Page 37 — Nouns

Q1 **a)** These nouns are words that name a type of person or thing. — common nouns
b) These nouns are the names of particular people and places (amongst other things). — proper nouns
c) These nouns are words for groups of things. — collective nouns

Q2

Common Nouns	Proper Nouns	Collective Nouns
pizza	February	horde of barbarians
cartoon	Robert	bunch of grapes
piano	Australia	bouquet of flowers

Q3 Proper nouns always start with a capital letter.

Q4 You should have circled: comfort, honesty, freedom, dream, desire, wealth and forgiveness.

Q5

					L		H			
	H	A	P	P	I	N	E	S	S	
			A		T		R			
			C		T		D			
L	U	C	K		E					
					R	U	M	O	U	R

Page 38 — Articles

Q1 **a)** Use 'a' or 'an' for general things.
b) Use 'a' before general things that sound like they begin with a consonant.
c) Use 'an' before general things that sound like they begin with a vowel.
d) Use 'the' for specific things.

Q2 **a)** I got a new coat for my birthday.
b) Martin went on the London Eye.
c) The spider in the bath is stuck.
d) The President of the Committee came.
e) A time machine would be useful.
f) There was a wasp's nest in the roof.

Q3 **a)** I saw a pig fly over the house.
b) Barcelona is a European city.
c) Jay was over an hour late.
d) The children built an igloo.

Answers

Q4 On the way to school, Finley saw the mayor of Stoatley land in a helicopter near the centre of the village. Its propellers made an extremely loud noise as they whirled round. After a few minutes, the helicopter's door opened and the mayor got out. He was wearing an enormous top hat, a pinstriped suit and an orange bow tie. Suddenly, the wind from the propellers blew the mayor's hat off and it landed right on top of Finley's head.

Q5 There is a theme park in Susie's town. It has a roller coaster, a haunted house, dodgems and a ghost train. The roller coaster is the highest in the country, and the ghost train is an extremely scary ride.

Page 39 — Pronouns

Q1

Personal Pronouns		
we	she	it
they		

Possessive Pronouns		
his	ours	mine
theirs	its	yours

Q2 **a)** He hates it.
b) They scare them.
c) She invites her.
d) This is yours.
e) Those are hers.
f) His shirt is very nice.

Q3

Pronouns Doing an Action	Pronouns Being Acted On	Possessive Pronouns
I	me	mine
he	him	his
you	you	yours

Q4 **a)** The kids and I went to the swimming pool.
b) Give me the packet of sweets or the teddy bear gets it!
c) Frances, Kevin, Farah and I are all going to the theatre.
d) It's time you and I had a little chat.

Page 40 — Pronouns

Q5 **a)** This is confusing because it isn't clear if Jimmy crushed the fly or the sandwich.
It would be clearer to write:
Jimmy crushed the fly that was on his sandwich.
(Or any similar answer where it is clear what Jimmy crushed.)
b) This is confusing because it isn't clear whether the students are asking if they can help the staff, or if the students are asking the staff to help them.
It would be clearer to write:
The students asked if the staff could help them.
(Or any similar answer where it is clear who needs help.)

Q6 **a)** I think the man who cleans the windows is called Trevor.
b) Charlie doesn't know which hat to buy.
c) To whom are you writing?
d) The clouds which are floating over Millomswick are soft and fluffy.
e) The story is about a prince who falls in love with a princess.
f) The person with whom I was speaking was very rude.
g) Karan's paintings, which sell like hot cakes, are on display in the town hall.

Q7 **a)** I don't know whose dog won.
b) Where's the man who's speaking?
c) Who's that over there?
d) Does anyone know whose jacket this is?

Page 41 — Verbs

Q1 You should have circled:
take, drive, go, laugh and are.

Q2 **a)** I am happy.
b) You are tall.
c) He is handsome.
d) She is silly.
e) It is annoying.
f) We are the best.
g) They are nervous.

Q3 There are some cows that lives in the field just outside our house. They walks down our road every Tuesday, when the farmer move them from one field to the other. The neighbours always watches from their windows to see what are going on.

Normally, the cows hardly ever stops, but whenever they do, they always eats Mum's flowers. Once this starts to happen, nothing can get them to move, unless it rain. They does not like to get wet because the rain make their hooves go cold.

Correct Verb Agreements:

live
walk
moves
watch
is
stop
eat
rains
do
makes

Q4 **a)** past tense
b) present tense
c) present tense
d) future tense
e) past tense
f) future tense

Page 42 — Adjectives

Q1 **a)** Some pupils think that homework is tedious, time-consuming and pointless.
b) However, teachers believe that homework is essential, educational and beneficial.
c) Fast food is often described as greasy, fattening and flavourless.
d) I like horror movies because they are terrifying, tense and grotesque.
e) My gran thinks that pop music is repetitive, tuneless and manufactured.
f) Other people believe pop music is rhythmical and harmonious.
g) Active people enjoy sport because it's invigorating, competitive and athletic.

Q2 Any sentences where at least two suitable adjectives have been added with the correct punctuation.

E.g.
a) The loud, bossy girl shouted.
b) The fast, silver car crashed.
c) The sad, lonely boy cried.
d) The calm, quiet baby slept.
e) The grumpy, ferocious alligator snapped.

Answers

Q3 **a)** The monster was tall, green and angry.
b) Chris eats smooth, rich, dark chocolate with crunchy, salty crisps.
c) She's wearing an extra large, bright pink, woolly jumper.
d) I like quiet, tidy, clever housemates who appreciate good, wholesome, tasty, home-made food.
e) Karin borrowed my extra long, pale blue, broken necklace.

Page 43 — Adverbs

Q1

Adverbs
quite soon readily happily firstly

Adjectives
annoying curly jolly saintly

Q2 **a)** The birds flew gracefully.
The adverb 'gracefully' tells you how the birds flew.
b) Vampires never look in mirrors.
The adverb 'never' tells you how often vampires look in mirrors.
c) Today we're going to the cinema.
The adverb 'today' tells you when we're going to the cinema.

Q3 **a)** We left the house quietly. (noisily or loudly)
b) They quickly ran through the park. (slowly)
c) The horse was behaving very strangely. (normally)
d) Janice filled in the form incorrectly. (correctly)
e) Patreese occasionally goes to the cinema. (usually, regularly or frequently)

Q4 **a)** They completed the test *with great ease.* ✓
b) We ran out onto the playing field *as quickly as possible.* ✓
c) *Under the barrel*, there is a mouse. ☐
d) Wendy could see a house at the end *of the lonely street.* ☐

Q5 **a)** Adjective
b) Adjective
c) Adverb

Page 44 — Sentence Structure

Q1 **a)** I asked her to phone me as soon as she arrived.
b) Please let us know when you plan to move in.
c) How would you like it if it happened to you?
d) These are the things you'll need: pyjamas, underwear and soap.
e) I don't know why he bought me a present — I didn't get him one.
f) Having read their postcard, I wish I'd been there.

Q2 **Suggested Answer**:
The unfortunate animal was eventually found in its hiding place, which was halfway up a tree at the bottom of the garden. It was brought back down after a neighbour lent an extra long ladder. The ladder was only just long enough to reach the cat, which by now was absolutely terrified.
(Or any similar answer with correct punctuation and grammar.)

Q3 **a)** Long sentences are fine as long as your meaning is clear. ✓
b) Often a short sentence is clearer and more effective than a long one. ✓
c) The longer the sentence, the more impressed the examiner will be. ☐
d) If you get lost halfway through writing a sentence, your reader will get lost too. ✓

Page 45 — Phrases and Clauses

Q1 **a)** Dad's trousers [P]
b) Tim wears purple trousers ☐
c) The trousers on the flag pole [P]
d) The terrible trousers [P]
e) I like trousers ☐
f) My other camouflage trousers [P]

Q2

Sentence	Phrase	Clause
The Martians invaded **on Tuesday morning**.	✓	
I met a gerbil on the way to school.		✓
A clown came for tea at our house.		✓
Jude fell on the floor **with a loud crash**.	✓	
During the beard festival, moustaches were banned.	✓	

Q3

Column A	Column B
Whilst I was waiting for the bus,	Bob's car splashed me.
Shouting as loud as I could,	I tried desperately to get his attention.
Although I was feeling hungry,	I hated the thought of eating a horse.

Q4 **a)** Column B
b) Column B
c) Column A
d) Column B

Page 46 — Phrases and Clauses

Q5 Any sentences where prepositional phrases have been added correctly.
E.g.
a) The yeti shouted in the street.
b) A spaceship crashed into the church wall.
c) Mike's mum laughed outside the school.
d) The alligator snapped at the zoo keeper.

Q6

Sentence	Main	Subordinate
I ate my breakfast before I went to bed.	✓	
When I watch a film, I always eat a big bag of popcorn.		✓
Maisy couldn't play football **because she had lost her boots**.		✓
Our plumber, who is very tall, **hit his head on the ceiling**.	✓	

Q7

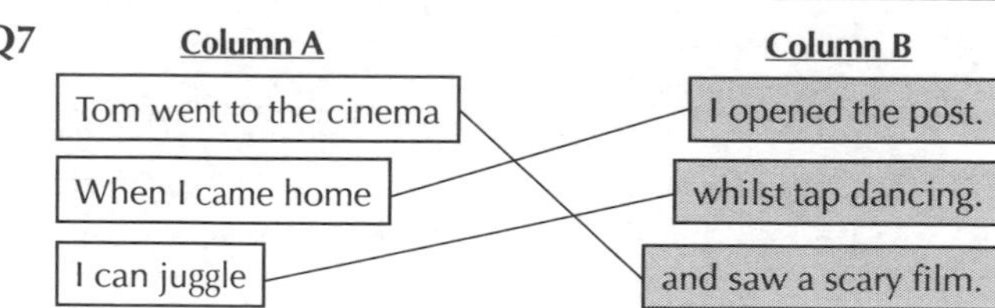

'Tom went to the cinema and saw a scary film' is a compound sentence.
'When I came home I opened the post' is a complex sentence.
'I can juggle whilst tap dancing' is a complex sentence.

Q8 Any sentences where relative clauses have been added correctly.
E.g.
a) The frog was blue, which was very unusual.
b) Henry wanted to see Daniel, who was his best friend.
c) In America they play baseball, which is a bit like rounders.
d) Diana laughed at Kerry, who was pretending to be a monkey.

Answers

Page 47 — Phrases and Clauses

Q9 a) <u>Keen to fly to Mars</u>, Roy fired up the rocket ship.
b) <u>Speaking from his heart</u>, he showed how he really felt.
c) I do a sun dance around the kitchen <u>whenever it rains</u>.
d) The DVD, <u>which I bought yesterday</u>, was actually a VDD (Very Dusty Disc).

Q10 Any sentences where conjunctions have been added correctly to make complex sentences.

E.g.
a) The dog growled at the man <u>as it moved closer to him</u>.
b) <u>Although she was wearing her favourite dress</u>, Sabrina chose to walk to the party.
c) I've run out of shampoo, <u>even though I bought two bottles last week</u>.

Q11 a) While chopping onions, he wears his goggles.
b) The teachers ran out to their cars as soon as the bell rang.
c) Beppe stayed calm despite meeting an elf.
d) Unless you're wearing pink, you can't come to the party.

Page 48 — Prepositions

Q1 a) The picture frame is <u>above the chair</u>.
b) The rat is <u>under the table</u>.
c) The lamp is <u>on the table</u>.
d) The teddy is <u>in front of the chair</u>.
e) The girl is <u>behind the chair</u>.
f) The table is <u>next to the chair</u>.

Q2 To begin your tour of Garrenberg, you need to first head <u>towards</u> the city centre. The quickest way to get to the centre is to go via the marketplace. Walking through the marketplace can be hectic, and you need to watch out for pickpockets, who are often hidden <u>amongst</u> the crowds.

Alternatively, you could take a longer walk and go around the outside of the city walls. <u>Between</u> 13 and 16 AD, a horde of barbarians launched an attack <u>against</u> the city, which was responsible for much of the damage that is visible today.

If you have time, you should look <u>around</u> the palace, and visit the royal chapel, where the royal tombs are buried right <u>beneath</u> your feet. Walk <u>across</u> the chapel square to find the palace café, which is open from 10 am to 4 pm <u>during</u> the day, and from 6 pm to 9 pm in the evening.

<u>Opposite</u> the palace gates, the city's main shopping street is <u>within</u> easy reach. Here you can buy postcards, souvenirs and local produce. Or you might like to climb <u>aboard</u> a boat and enjoy a city cruise <u>along</u> the River Mo.

Page 49 — Conjunctions

Q1 a) Two or more main clauses joined together with one of the FANBOYS conjunctions. — compound sentence
b) A sentence with two or more ideas joined by a conjunction which isn't one of the FANBOYS. — complex sentence
c) A sentence with one main clause. — simple sentence

Q2 a) <u>While</u> wearing a feather hat, my nose started to itch.
b) She remained calm <u>until</u> I ran up and down screaming "Emergency!"
c) It was dark in the cellar <u>before</u> we turned the lights on.
d) <u>After</u> Mark had gone to the shops, I raided the biscuit tin.
e) My dad has learnt to juggle <u>since</u> he joined the circus.

Q3 a) Rajwant runs on Wednesdays, <u>and</u> plays tennis on Mondays. (<u>Compound</u>)
b) Rajwant runs <u>because</u> he likes to keep fit. (<u>Complex</u>)
c) Rajwant runs in circles. (<u>Simple</u>)
d) Rajwant runs to work <u>if</u> he gets up late. (<u>Complex</u>)
e) Rajwant runs every day, <u>yet</u> he is still unfit. (<u>Compound</u>)

Q4 a) <u>Since</u> the band was quite loud, Ben couldn't hear me.
b) Tanya went up the ladder <u>while</u> Danny watched from below.
c) <u>Although</u> the maggots were on offer, Maggie didn't buy any.
d) The boy band 'Three Projection' came to town, <u>so</u> I went to their concert.

Page 50 — Conjunctions

Q5 a) We could either go to the gym <u>or</u> we could play tennis.
b) The music in the disco was awful, <u>but</u> / <u>yet</u> we still had fun.
c) The chocolate cake was yummy, <u>and</u> the blueberry muffins were delicious.
d) We couldn't get tickets for the match, <u>so</u> / <u>but</u> we watched it on TV instead.

Q6 Any sentences where the conjunctions have been used correctly.

E.g.
a) <u>Despite</u> the cold weather, dad refused to put the heating on.
b) I get hungry <u>whenever</u> I watch cookery shows.
c) <u>Although</u> he prefers swimming, Eli is better at running.
d) Racing is fun to watch, <u>whereas</u> snooker is just boring.

Q7 Linda likes to spend her evenings curled up on the couch in front of the TV, <u>whereas</u> Roy likes to go to bed early.

<u>Although</u> Roy likes a cooked breakfast in the morning, he always gets up too late and <u>therefore</u> has to have cereal instead. <u>However</u>, Linda is always up early and she takes the dog for a walk <u>until</u> Roy finally gets out of bed. <u>Whilst</u> Roy is in the shower, Linda reads the newspaper, <u>whereas</u> the dog goes back to bed.

<u>In spite of</u> starting work earlier than Roy, Linda can leave the house later, <u>since</u> she doesn't have to travel as far as he does. <u>Consequently</u> Roy sets off 15 minutes before Linda. <u>While</u> Linda and Roy go out to work, the dog waits in her bed for the postman to arrive. The dog will often fall back to sleep. <u>Nevertheless</u>, she always hears the sound of the postman arriving.

Answers

Page 51 — Conjunctions

Q8 **a)** The guest of honour failed to arrive; however, the party went ahead as planned.
b) The spy waited until the coast was clear.
c) Joanne booked her flights as soon as the hotel booking was confirmed.
d) The science lab exploded as a result of the experiment going wrong.

Q9 Words which put an **opposite / different view**: however, in spite of this, nevertheless, despite this

Words to say **more of the same**, or to **back up** what you've just written: furthermore, moreover

Words to write about something which **happened because of** the thing you've just written about: consequently, therefore

Words to write about something which **happened at a later time**: later, afterwards

Page 52 — Paragraphs

Q1 I once knew a boy who would only eat chocolate cake. He was very particular about what kind of chocolate cake he would eat — cakes with butter icing were okay, but he refused to eat any chocolate cakes with fudge or cherry in them.

We first met in Year 7, and I love chocolate, so I knew we would be friends straightaway.

However, by the time we were in Year 9, I started to find him really annoying. I had grown sick of the smell of chocolate, and sick of the sight of him.

Nowadays I live in a different town, so I rarely see him. I often wonder whether or not he still only eats chocolate cake.

Q2 My great grandmother is just about to turn one hundred. She is an amazing woman who's still really active, despite her age; but she is also very difficult to please.

Last year, to celebrate her ninety-ninth birthday, my whole family stayed at the King Richard Hotel. We had a big, expensive dinner, and then stayed the night so that no one would have to drive. Everyone had a great time, except my great grandmother, who complained that the jelly wasn't wobbly enough, and the ice cream was too icy.

We're going to Paris for her hundredth birthday, which is an amazing birthday treat. I don't think she can possibly find anything to complain about in the beautiful French capital.

I've just remembered — she hates flying, so maybe Paris isn't the best idea after all.

Q3 In the 19th century, women did not have the same rights as men. One of the main differences was that women did not have the right to vote. This resulted in a campaign for women's suffrage (the right to vote).

There were two main groups of protesters — the Suffragists and the Suffragettes. The Suffragists focused on peaceful protests, whilst the Suffragettes were more violent. They burned down churches, chained themselves to railings and sometimes even attacked politicians.

Emmeline Pankhurst was perhaps the most famous campaigner, and she was renowned for her courage. Sadly, Pankhurst died in June 1928, just weeks before all women over 21 were given the right to vote.

The Suffragette movement was extremely important in British politics, although many people still believe that there are not enough women in politics today.

Page 53 — Paragraphs

Q4 The Swamp Martians live in a quagmire on the top of Misty Moor. It is a lonely, boggy place, full of foul smells and strange creatures.

Mrs Waterweed, head of the Swamp Martian clan, tries her best to make life in the quagmire comfortable, whether it means filling the house with flowers, or cooking her famous eel and marsh gas soup — an activity she was currently engaged in.

Over in a neighbouring bog, her husband, Mr Waterweed, was fishing for eels. Whilst fishing, he kept an eye out for 'Gobbling Goo' — a type of mud which could suck him up if he wasn't careful.

"Dinner's ready," Mrs Waterweed suddenly cried.

An hour later, both the Waterweeds sat back in their chairs feeling happy and well-fed.

Q5 I started the second paragraph because a new character was introduced.
I started the third paragraph because a new location was introduced.
I started the fourth paragraph because someone new started speaking.
I started the fifth paragraph because a new time was introduced.

Page 54 — Negatives

Q1 **a)** You're definitely going to win. OR You've got no chance of losing.
b) The aliens can't find anywhere to land.
c) Barry doesn't think anyone will come.
d) The lads don't have anything to be afraid of.
e) Ivan has three sweets, but Drew doesn't have any.
f) Arthur and Merlin don't need any help.

Q2 **a)** Abdul wants some sweets, but Gillian has not got any.
b) I have not got anything to lose.
c) Tom wants a day off, but that is not going to happen.
d) I am not dyeing my hair green and Charlie is not shaving his beard off.
e) The Johnsons have not got any pets.
f) Irene has not finished her work yet.

Page 55 — Mixed Questions

Q1 **a)** verb
b) main clause
c) adverb
d) noun
e) adjective
f) subordinate clause
g) preposition
h) article

Q2 Any two verbs from: went, was, didn't pack, had, make

Answers

Any two articles from:
a, an, the
Any two adverbs from:
yesterday, absolutely
Any two common nouns from:
trip, boat, day, supplies, snacks, canal
Any two prepositions from:
for, on, along
Any two adjectives from:
jolly, gorgeous, narrow

Q3 **a)** interference **e)** participation
b) existence **f)** complication
c) dedication **g)** elevation
d) persistence **h)** reference

Page 56 — Mixed Questions

Q4

a)	A verb	✓	f)	An object	☐
b)	A preposition	☐	g)	At least one capital letter	✓
c)	A subject	✓	h)	It needs to be a statement	☐
d)	It contains a complete idea	✓	i)	At least four words	☐
e)	Punctuation	✓	j)	At least two clauses	☐

Q5 **E.g.**
a) Sally didn't see the mess on the floor until she stepped in it.
b) I hate the feel of toothpaste on my tongue, whereas I love the feel of mouthwash.
c) Mike forgot to get some petrol at the weekend, and hence he couldn't drive to work.
d) The cat couldn't eat its tea because it had eaten too many biscuits in the morning.
e) Phil and Ben kept smiling, even though they were having a bad day at the office.
f) United fans always sing loudly at matches wherever they go.
(Or any sentences where a prepositional phrase has been added correctly.)

Page 57 — Mixed Questions

Q6 **a)** Ulrich doesn't know me, and Karl doesn't know me either.
b) You don't own a car, and Riony doesn't own a bike.
c) Stuart and Elaine don't have a cat, and we don't have a dog.
d) Lillian doesn't want to come shopping, but I don't like shopping on my own.

Q7 On Wednesday Malcolm is celebrating his sixteenth birthday, so he and I are going to the cinema. We thought about inviting Emily, but she's going on holiday to France that day and can't come. However, I'm sure we'll have a great time anyway.

I've already bought his present, which is going to be a big surprise. It's a navy blue football shirt with the number three on the back — that's his lucky number. He's not a big football fan, but when he was talking to Liam, who's mad about the sport, Malcolm said he'd like a football shirt. I can't wait to see him open his present — he's not going to have any idea what it is.

Section Four — Grammar: Tenses

Page 58 — Writing About Now

Q1 **a)** He says **f)** You complain
b) I know **g)** It seems
c) We play **h)** We show
d) They make **i)** I tell
e) She takes

Q2 **a)** Stanley flies to New York every year.
b) Ron catches the bus to work.
c) Our grandpa goes to night school.
d) Houri passes the ball to Greg.
e) Ann fries the bacon in the morning.
f) Clive does his exercises every day.

Q3 Rob has a fear of cucumbers. His friends say he should really do something about it, but Rob thinks his friends are just silly. He knows he can control his fear by simply avoiding cucumbers, and he does just that.

Page 59 — Writing About Now

Q4

Present Tense	'-ing Form'
He talks	He is talking
They help	They are helping
I ask	I am asking
It melts	It is melting

Present Tense	'-ing Form'
They sleep	They are sleeping
It rains	It is raining
We keep	We are keeping
I eat	I am eating

Q5 The annual Galaxy Gala is in full swing, but it's all going wrong. The balloons are popping, the waiters are dropping the dishes, a Venus Vole is digging holes in the floor, and dangerous Mars Mutants are tapping at the door to be let in. The guests are not happy and the organiser is offering everyone refunds.

Q6 **a)** The scouts are tying knots in their leader's shoelaces.
b) Cassie is battling to keep her eyes open.
c) Jaden and Terese are dyeing their hair.

Page 60 — Writing About the Past

Q1

Verbs	The Simple Past
talk	talked
hope	hoped
doubt	doubted
ask	asked
work	worked

Verbs	The Simple Past
tease	teased
offer	offered
practise	practised
play	played
behave	behaved

Q2 **a)** I gave **h)** We spilt / spilled
b) He was **i)** I copied
c) We took **j)** They built
d) They slept **k)** You saw
e) It travelled **l)** He grew
f) She kept **m)** It swept
g) You told **n)** She heard

Q3 Yesterday we made a birthday card for Granny. We cut shapes out of paper and stuck them onto some card. Dad bought her a present and Mum hid it behind the sofa. They wrote clues for Granny to follow, and she quickly found the present.

Answers

Page 61 — The Past Tense with Have

Q1

Verbs	Past with 'have'
She eats	She has eaten
It is	It has been
They go	They have gone
I arrive	I have arrived
We give	We have given

Verbs	Past with 'have'
He finishes	He has finished
You write	You have written
We have	We have had
It takes	It has taken
I show	I have shown

Q2 **a)** I have been to see the doctor.
b) We have done a great job.
c) They have not done the washing-up.
d) Caleb has seen the new Jenny Pond film.
e) I have done my best.
f) We have been living here for ages.

Q3 **a)** Jeff knows of a nice café.
b) They should have been in bed.
c) I could have been a film star.
d) Mel might have joined in.
e) I thought of a possible plan.
f) She should have known better.

Page 62 — Staying in the Right Tense

Q1 **a)** On Tuesday we had a buffet and we played board games.
b) Yesterday the superhero saved the President and rescued his cat.
c) I am keen to learn Spanish and have decided to take lessons. OR I was keen to learn Spanish and had decided to take lessons.
d) My printer had broken and so I needed to go shopping. OR My printer has broken and so I need to go shopping.
e) The sales are on, so I am going to the shops right now.

Q2 Last Saturday, Hootle Village Hall held its annual autumn fair. There was a car boot sale, which offered clothes and toys; there was a cake stall, which sold a selection of bakery items; and there was a face-painting stand. A raffle also took place, and for the children there was a line-dancing competition. The mayor also came, and he helped to run some of the stands. The fair raised over £300 for the local community.

Page 63 — Mixed Questions

Q1 **a)** I am in Spain for my holiday.
b) We play / are playing catch with the neighbours.
c) I walk / am walking from the church to the circus.
d) I don't know what he is.

Q2 **a)** The spy spoke five languages.
b) They only bought meat from the butcher's.
c) I was on the school's netball team, and I played squash.
d) Kelsey listened to the radio and whistled along.

Q3 **a)** Harvey thought a lot about taking over the world.
b) Samia has passed her exam with flying colours.
c) Norris and his horse are winning the race.
d) Stella takes / is taking her sister to ballet lessons.

Page 64 — Mixed Questions

Q4

Present Tense	Present '-ing' Form	Simple Past	Past Tense with 'have'
He goes	He is going	He went	He has gone
We see	We are seeing	We saw	We have seen
They take	They are taking	They took	They have taken
I begin	I am beginning	I began	I have begun

Q5 Last week, the headmaster at Piggleswick High School turned his school into a giant jungle gym for a day. He replaced the stairs with inflatable slides and put a bouncy castle in the hall. To get out of the staff room, the teachers had to use a fireman's pole. The headmaster also built a fort out of plastic bricks in the dining room. All the pupils thought it was a great idea.

Today, it's the pupils' turn to decorate the school. Right now, they are blowing up balloons and hanging streamers in the classrooms. The head girl is making party hats while the prefects are baking food for a buffet.

Section Five — Writing Skills

Page 65 — Writing in Standard English

Q1 **a)** True
b) True
c) True
d) False
e) True
f) False

Q2

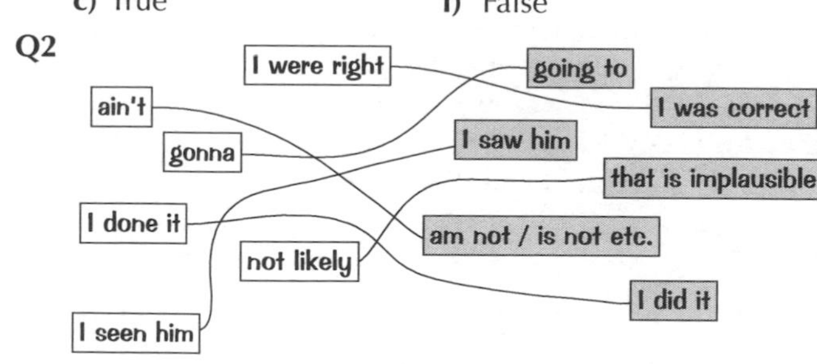

Q3
a) Writing to apply to be an astronaut ✓
b) Shouting to a friend to pass you the ball ☐
c) Showing parents around your school ✓
d) Writing a letter to the Prime Minister ✓
e) Giving a tourist directions ✓
f) Arguing over what to watch at your friend's house ☐

Page 66 — Writing in Standard English

Q4 **a)** I did really well — I think I did better than last time.
b) The man that came yesterday was very strange.
c) We waited / were waiting for a long time, but we didn't see / never saw him.
d) I asked him if I could borrow / if he would lend me his pen and he gave it to me.

Answers

e) It doesn't have to be like this — we don't have to argue.
f) I didn't do anything — it wasn't me who broke it.

Q5

Standard English	Non-Standard English
This is a real example.	He is well good at chess.
We never knew why.	I'd like them biscuits.
This is not proper behaviour.	I have wrote them a letter.
The essay is well written.	I should of known better.
There were none left.	I was proper glad.

Page 67 — Writing in Standard English

Q6 a) They go out all the time.
b) I did it right the first time.
c) I don't know if they are here.
d) I thought he was coming.
e) That was terrifying.
f) I have been away.
g) They have given us gifts.
h) It was the best party ever.

Q7 Suggested Answer:

When we were children, people weren't allowed to waste anything. We made everything last a long time. Our mum would scold us for throwing away anything that might still be useful. She would watch us to make sure we had eaten everything that she gave us. Rationing meant you had to be really inventive with the cooking. Yet no one ever said they didn't like something, not even Alice.

In those days we didn't have any modern vacuum cleaners or washing machines. We wouldn't have had money for anything like that. But you would never have heard anyone complaining. I haven't known anything like it since.

(Or any similar answer with correct Standard English.)

Page 68 — Writing in the Right Style

Q1

Formal	Informal
politician's speech job application school science report	e-mail to a friend text message to a friend postcard to your cousin

Q2 a) Very formal
b) Fairly informal
c) Very informal
d) Quite formal

Q3

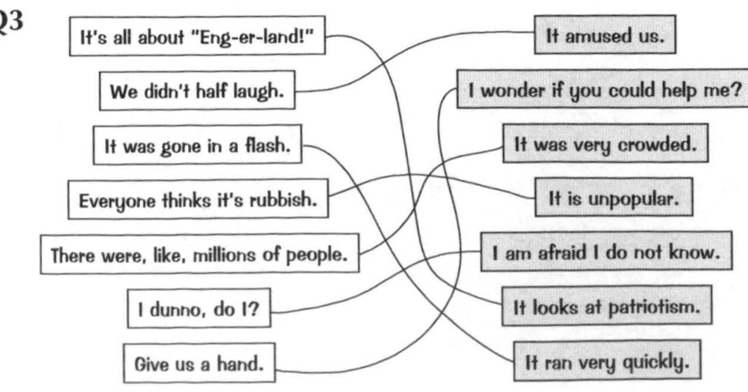

Page 69 — Writing in the Right Style

Q4 a) Formal
b) Formal
c) Informal
d) Informal
e) Informal
f) Formal

Q5 a) The England manager said he was gutted about their defeat.
b) It looks like it will rain cats and dogs on Saturday.
c) The ladies yakked to each other on the phone for an hour.
d) When Duncan asked for the day off, his boss told him to get lost.
e) Mrs Gladding's dishwasher had conked out, so she called the plumber.
f) The film tracks his relationship with his girlfriend, and ends when she dumps him.

Q6 Dear Mr Spudwrangler,

I am writing to inform you that I recently had an appalling meal at one of your Spudwrangler restaurants. The waiters were impolite, and the food was tasteless.

I hope that you will endeavour to make things right. I look forward to your response.

Yours sincerely,
Toby Brown

Page 70 — Writing in the Right Style

Q7 Suggested Answers:

a) He said it was not very good.
b) Please could you pass me a packet of crisps? Thank you.
c) Your mother's going to be furious with you for the state of your shoes.
d) The criminal said he had not stolen the car or anything else.
e) Vincent van Gogh was a famous artist who became so depressed he sliced his ear off.
f) In Shakespeare's time people were constantly ill and many people suffered from the plague.
(Or any similar answers written in a correct formal style.)

Q8 Suggested Answer:

Just thought I'd drop you a line to let you know that I'm having a fantastic holiday with my mates. I've done loads of sunbathing, and even got round to doing some cultural stuff as well. It's a shame you couldn't make it. I hope everything is good with you. I can't wait to see you soon.

(Or any similar answer written in an informal style.)

Page 71 — Writing in the Right Style

Q9 Suggested Answer:

The Shetland Islands are a group of islands to the north-east of the Orkneys. In the 9th century the Vikings invaded and took over the islands. The Vikings held on to the islands until 1471, when Scotland seized control of them. The Shetland Islands' history means their culture is a mixture of Norse and Scottish traditions.

Answers

Most of the Shetland Islands' economy is driven by fishing, but the islands are also famous for Shetland Ponies.
(Or similar answer written in a correct formal style.)

Q10 a) The statue was unveiled by the mayor.
b) Residents were shocked by the decision to close the library.
c) Local artists were commissioned by the council.

These sentences seem more formal because they are written in the passive voice.

Page 72 — Choosing Active or Passive

Q1

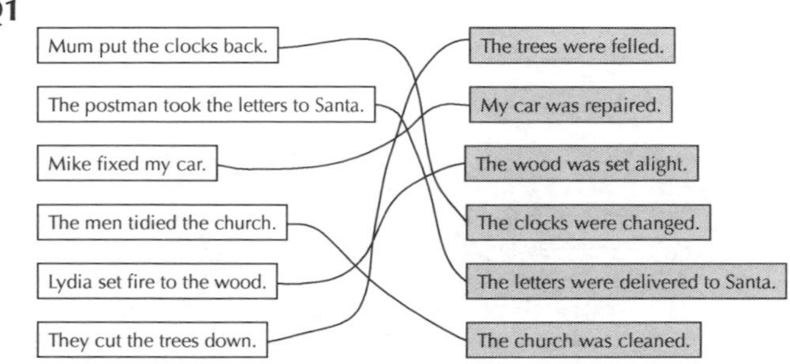

Q2 a) The vase was broken.
b) She was let down.
c) The boat was torpedoed.
d) The house was broken into.
e) The important message was forgotten.

Q3 a) Ana was awarded the 'Best Baker' prize by the judges.
b) The experiment was carried out by me on Tuesday.
c) The mosque was built in 1934 by a lot of people.
d) Some sugar was added to the mixture by us.
e) The train was delayed by trees on the line.

Page 73 — Choosing Active or Passive

Q4 a) We have already discussed this subject.
b) They introduced a new system.
c) Several famous people visited the school.
d) The servants cleaned the whole house.
e) He admired her.
f) I washed their hair and scrubbed their faces.

Q5 a) Passive
b) Active
c) Active
d) Passive
e) Passive

Q6 a) (Ian) held the racquets.
b) (Ishram) was seen by the guard.
c) (The competitors) were warned by the referee.
d) (Marianne) ordered a kebab.

Page 74 — Spelling Tips

Q1 Suggested Answers:
a) Rhythm Has Your Two Hips Moving.
b) Never Eat Chips — Eat Salad Sandwiches And Remain Young.
c) I Make Mistakes Eavesdropping Daily — I Aspire To Eavesdrop Like You.
(Or any mnemonic that tells you the letters in the correct order.)

Q2 Any answers that help you remember the spelling of the words.
E.g.
a) develop ment
b) further more
c) embarrass ing
d) accommodat ion
e) relat ive
f) inter nation al
g) un fashion ably
h) un fortun ate ly

Q3

'qu'	'ough'	'gu'
antique	drought	guest
quality	nought	guitar
banquet	tough	fatigue
queen	thorough	tongue

Page 75 — Spelling Tips

Q4

```
Y X W N I E G H B U R A A
V U T O S R Q P O A D R C
N M L I K J I H G D F U C
W E N S D A Y E R R D O O
Y L A A B A Z E Y E X B M
A D Y D W Y S U T S R H M
D I B O Q S P D N S M G O
S S O M R A E P P A S I D
E A U M L K J I H G N E A
N P R O R U B H G I E N T
D E F C D I S A P E A R I
E E E C Y A D S D N E W O
W R C A D R R E S S B A N
```

Q5 a) There's a rat in separate.
b) There's a lie in belief.
c) You gain when you get a bargain.
d) The secretary has a secret.
e) Emma faced a dilemma.

Q6 a) separate
b) belief
c) bargain
d) secretary
e) dilemma

Q7 Answers may vary.

Page 76 — Mixed Questions

Q1 a) They haven't got any choice.
b) Harvey and I are giving it our best shot.
c) I'm really angry about those robberies.

Q2 a) Neville stole fifty pounds.
b) That would have been very expensive.

Q3

Active Sentence	Passive Sentence
Anna wrote the poem.	The poem was written by Anna.
You saw him.	He was seen by you.
A little elf bit me.	I was bitten by a little elf.
The teacher caught us.	We were caught by the teacher.

Q4 Yesterday the teachers treated the pupils at Blackhaven School to a party. The secretary booked a band, and the headmistress invited guests to attend. The janitor banned fizzy pop, but the deputy head encouraged the pupils to bring their own food.

ISBN 978 1 78294 116 3
9 781782 941163

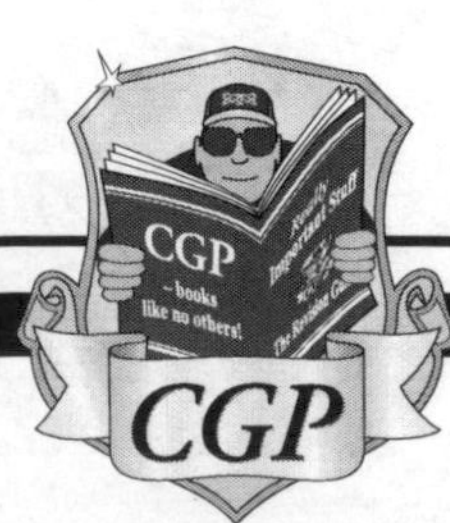

EGA31
£2.00
(Retail Price)

www.cgpbooks.co.uk